SWORD ART ONLINE
GIRLS' OPS
001
ART: NEKO NEKOBYO
ORIGINAL STORY: REKI KAWAHAR
CHARACTER DESIGN: ab

001

SWORD ART ONLINE
GIRLS' OPERATIONS

art: Neko Nekobyou
original story: Reki Kawahara
character design: abec

C o n t e n t s

SWORD ART ONLINE GIRLS' OPS 001

SWORD ART ONLINE
GIRLS' OPERATIONS

ART: NEKO NEKOBYOU
ORIGINAL STORY: REKI KAWAHARA
CHARACTER DESIGN: abec

STAGE. 1
PINA!!
PINA, HANG IN THERE!
HUFF!
HUFF!
GUTA (SLUMP)
HUFF!
OOOOO (WHOOSH)
PINA!
DON'T LEAVE ME ALL ALONE...
GA (TRIP)
EEK!

OO (WHOOSH)
ZAN (SLASH)
HELP...!
GYU (CLENCH)

サァァァ
SAAA
(FWOOSH)

FUWA
(BEAM)

PWEE!
KIRITO-
SAN!
PI
(BEEP)

ピ
PI (BEEP)
ピ
PI
ピ
PI
ピ
PI
ピ
PI
ピ
PI
カチッ
KACHI (CLICK)
YAWN!
...MM.
WEIRD. I FEEL LIKE I JUST WOKE UP FROM A NIGHTMARE...
BUT...I'M NOT IN A BAD MOOD ABOUT IT?
SILICA
REAL NAME: KEIKO AYANO

UROWW.
GOOD MORNING...
...PINA FROM THIS SIDE.
チュッ
CHU (SMOOCH)
UGH, STILL SLEEPY...
ピピ
PIPI (BEEP)
MOSO (RUSTLE)
モゾ
モゾ
MOSO

IS THIS...?
SAO RETURNEES SCHOOL
PATA
PATA (FLAP)
LIZ-SAN!
PATA
PATA
PATA
LIZ-SAN, DID YOU SEE THIS!?

THE NEW AINC...
STOP RIGHT THERE!
AUGH!
BISHI (JAB)
HOW MANY TIMES DO I HAVE TO TELL YOU? I'M NOT "LIZ" IN REAL LIFE, IT'S "RIKA"!
IT'S BAD MANNERS TO CALL ME BY MY ALIAS AT SCHOOL!
LISBETH REAL NAME: RIKA SHINOZAKI
GAYA (MURMUR)
AAH!
GAYA
GAYA
GAYA

I'm sorry, Rika-san.
I just keep doing it by accident.
KATA (THUMP)
AWW...
I KNOW, I KNOW.
IT'S REALLY HARD NOT TO JUST CALL YOU "SILICA THE DRAGON-TAMER."
DRINK THIS, AND CHILL OUT.
HRRM!
SHEESH!
I SAID I WAS SORRY!
I KNOW, SORRY.
THANK YOU.
SO, SHALL I GUESS WHAT YOU CAME TO TELL ME ABOUT?
NIKO (GRIN)
NIKO
GLUG GLUG

THE NEW AINCRAD ADD-ON QUEST, "ANGEL'S WHISPER RINGS"!
SO YOU SAW IT TOO!
I WANT ONE SO BAD!
BUT OF COURSE!
I WENT TO GET THEM IN SAO TOO.
THE RINGS ARE ONLY GIVEN TO THOSE WHO PASS THE ANGEL'S TRIAL.
AFTER ALL, IT SAYS THAT THOSE WHO TRADE THE RINGS FORM AN ETERNAL BOND.
YES, AND ON TOP OF THAT...

THOSE WHO HAVE TRADED RINGS...
...CAN SEND EACH OTHER VOICE MESSAGES ONCE A MONTH!
IT'S SO ROMANTIC!

SPEAKING OF WHICH, KAZUTO-SAN'S AWAY AT TANEGASHIMA ON THE STUDY PROGRAM.
I SENT HIM AN INVITATION, FORGETTING HE COULDN'T EVEN LOG IN.
YEAH, IT SUCKS.
WHY DOES HE HAVE TO BE AWAY, AND AT A TIME LIKE THIS?
PHOOEY...

AS A MATTER OF FACT, I GOT ONE FROM KIRI... KAZUTO-SAN ONCE.

HUH?

THOUGH HE JUST SEEMED TO THINK OF IT AS SOME KIND OF PHONE...

Sigh... That sounds like something he'd do.

HMM?

WAIT A MINUTE, KEIKO.
ARE YOU SAYING YOU REACHED OUT TO HIM BEFORE ME?
ZUI (LEAN)

YES. I MEAN, IT SAID THE ANGEL'S WHISPER RINGS QUEST GOT HARDER AFTER THE ALO TRANSFER UPDATE...
...SO I FIGURED IT WOULD BE TOO HARD FOR US.
WHAT ABOUT ASUNA-SAN? DO YOU THINK SHE'S AVAILABLE?

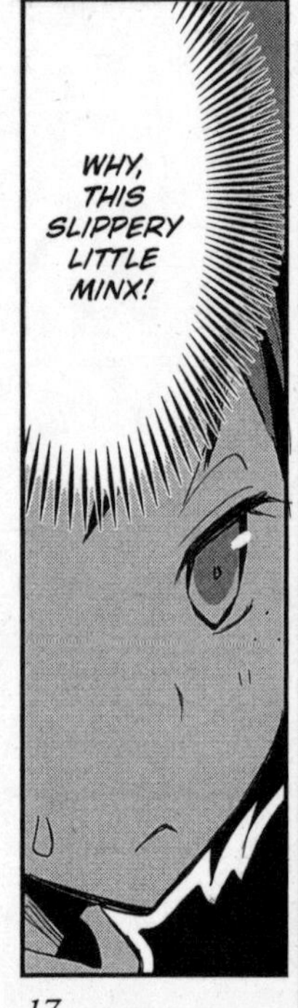
WHY, THIS SLIPPERY LITTLE MINX!

...ASUNA SEEMS TO BE GOING THROUGH A LOT AT HOME.

OH, I SEE. WELL, I CAN'T FORCE THE ISSUE...
WHAT ABOUT LEAFA? I'LL CALL SUGUHA-SAN.

PURURURU (RRRRR)
SHE MIGHT NOT BE FAMILIAR WITH ITEMS FROM SAO...
...BUT I'M SURE SHE'LL BE INTRIGUED WHEN I TELL HER WHAT THE RINGS DO.

PU (CLICK)
AH, SUGUHA-SAN?
HEY, CHECK THIS OUT!

THE ANGEL'S WHISPER RINGS!? WOW, THOSE SOUND SO COOL!

OF COURSE I'M IN!
LEAFA
REAL NAME:
SUGUHA KIRIGAYA
I'LL TOTALLY PASS THE HOLY ANGEL'S TRIAL TO GET THEM.
ETERNAL BONDS, HUH...?
I KNOW!
I'll get two and give one to Onii-chan... Heh-heh!

WELL, WE'LL SEE YOU...
...IN "ALFHEIM ONLINE"!

KYUUUN (ZWOOP)
LET'S GET THOSE ANGEL'S WHISPER RINGS!

OH MY DEAR GOOD-NESS.
KIRA (SPARKLE)
KIRA
YOU ACTUALLY PASSED THE TRIAL?
LAAAME.
YOU DON'T SERIOUSLY EXPECT ANYONE'S GOING TO BELIEVE IN SOME "ETERNAL BOND" NONSENSE JUST BECAUSE OF THIS MEASLY QUEST, DO YOU?
NEXT UP! GO DEFEAT THE DEMON LIVING IN THE "TOWER OF THE DOWN-TRODDEN"...
...AND SHOW ME THE STRENGTH OF YOUR BONDS OR WHATEVER.
QUEST NPC: ANGEL
HURRY UP! CHOP CHOP!

OKAY, I'VE TRIED TO WORK WITH THIS...
SHE SHOULD BE MORE AUSTERE AND DIGNIFIED!
...BUT THIS IS NOT THE ANGEL I IMAGINED!
IT'S HARD NOT TO FEEL THAT WAY.
SHE'S SUPPOSED TO BE BITTER BECAUSE SHE'S BEEN BETRAYED BY SO MANY HUMANS.
HER OUTFIT GOT ALTERED A BIT IN THE CONVERSION, BUT OTHERWISE SHE'S THE SAME.
A LITTLE TOO BITTER, IF YOU ASK ME!
OH, DON'T WORRY. SHE FOLLOWS THE TSUNDERE SCRIPT, SO SHE'LL BE NICE AND FRIENDLY BEFORE YOU KNOW IT.
RIGHT?
OF COURSE!
AWWW...
C'MON.

Hey.
HMPH!
I guess you might as well...
...be careful out there or whatever.
HA HA!
YOU'RE RIGHT. SHE REALLY IS GETTING NICER ALREADY...
I GUESS SHE'S NOT SO BAD...
KA (BLUSH)
GATAAN (SLAM)
PSYCHE!
D-DID YOU REALLY THINK I'D SAY THAT!? LOSER!
!?

LOSERRRS!
FU (FLIT)
AH.
GAAAAH!
SHE'S NOT A TSUNDERE! SHE'S JUST A SULKY CHILD!
LEAFA-CHAN'S REAC-TIONS...
...ARE SO FUN TO WATCH.

AUGH...
IS THIS THE KIND OF QUEST SAO IS STUFFED WITH?
THIS HAS COMPLETELY DESTROYED MY MENTAL IMAGE OF ANGELS...
PLENTY OF THEM ARE WEIRD, BUT THIS WAS DEFINITELY ONE OF THE MORE MEMORABLE QUESTS.
I MEAN, THE "DEMON" WE HAVE TO GO BEAT IS ACTUALLY A REALLY FLUFFY BUNNY.
KRURU-RU...

A BUNNY!? BUT DIDN'T SHE SAY IT WAS A DEMON?
YES, A BUNNY-SHAPED DEMON.
UKYU?
I COULD BARELY BELIEVE MY EYES WHEN I FIRST SAW IT.
A WINGED RABBIT! A LITTLE ON THE BIG SIDE.
SO CUTE!
BUT... HUGE!
GU (CLENCH)
LATER THE ANGEL SAID...
"I DIDN'T THINK IT WAS RIGHT TO THREATEN YOU WITH A BIG SCARY DEMON! Y-YOU GOT A PROBLEM WITH THAT?"
IT WAS A PRETTY WEAK EXCUSE.
IN FACT, IT WAS HARDER FOR ME TO BEAT UP ON A CUTE, FLUFFY BUNNY RABBIT.
IT WAS PRETTY TOUGH TOO.

THE TRUE "DERE" PART HAPPENS IN THE FINAL BATTLE!
SURE IT LOOKED SCARY, BUT WHENEVER YOU WERE ON THE ROPES, IT WOULD OCCASIONALLY THROW BUFFS ON YOU.
I KNEW IT WAS ACTUALLY THE ANGEL IN DISGUISE RIGHT AWAY.
WHAT!? THAT HAPPENED TO YOU?

IT NEVER DID THAT FOR ME WHEN I FOUGHT IT. I WONDER WHY?
YOU MUST HAVE DONE SOMETHING WRONG, SILICA.
DO YOU SUPPOSE THE ANGEL HAS AN AFFECTION PARAMETER OR SOMETHING?
MAYBE IF I'D BEEN A LITTLE BIT NICER, SHE WOULD HAVE SHOWN ME FAVOR...
BUT I DIDN'T DO ANYTHING!
HRRM...

ARRRGH!

GABA (WHOOSH)

GEEZ!

STOP THAT! I HAVEN'T DONE THIS QUEST YET!
GABAA (SQUISH)
NO SPOILERS, ALL RIGHT!? YOU CAN'T TALK ABOUT IT ON YOUR OWN EITHER!
HYA!
EEK!

SORRY, LEAFA, SORRY.
AWW...
WE'RE SORRY, LEAFA-SAN.

LOOK, I GET THAT IT'S A FUN MEMORY FOR YOU GUYS, BUT COME ON...
PUNI (BOOP)
LOOK WHO'S LONELY!

BASA (FLAP)
LOOK, THERE IT IS!
THAT'S THE "TOWER OF THE DOWN-TRODDEN"!
WITH THE THREE OF US, IT SHOULDN'T BE MUCH TROUBLE.
TIME FOR LEAFA-SAN TO HAVE SOME FUN WITH THAT CUDDLY-WUDDLY, FLUFFY WINGED BUNNY!
GII (CREAK)

DO
(BOOOM)

フシュウゥ
FUSHUUU
(FSHHH)

GUOOOO (GROAAAH)
GOKURI (GULP)
...Um...
WASN'T THE MONSTER SUPPOSED TO BE A CUTE BUNNY RABBIT UNLEASHED BY THE ANGEL!?
THAT'S WHAT IT SHOULD HAVE BEEN!

AH!
OF COURSE! THE UPDATE!
THEY SAID THE DIFFICULTY HAD BEEN UPGRADED AFTER THE ALO TRANSFER UPDATE...
THIS MUST BE WHAT THEY MEANT!
BUT WHY WOULD IT BE SO ACTIVE ALREADY, WITHOUT ANYONE ELSE AROUND...?
A BUG?
Well...
OH!
...!
ZA (ZSHH)

HYUO (WHOOSH)
ヒュオッ
KOHHHH (HRRRR)
コォオオオ
AN-OTHER PLAY-ER!?
SOMEONE ELSE GOT HERE BEFORE US...?
HUH!?

KIRITO-SAN!?
GO
(DOOM)

SWORD ART ONLINE
GIRLS' OPS

SILICA'S OUTFIT...
...IS KIND OF EMBAR-RASSING.
LISBETH + SILICA'S CLOTHES

STAGE 2
GO
(DOOM)
BAJIJI
(BZZZT)
...!
JII
ZUZAZA
(ZZSHH)

キュ!!
GYUII
(ZOOP)
AH!

KIRITO-SAN!?

DAN (WHOMP)
I DON'T KNOW WHAT'S GOING ON...
...BUT WE HAVE TO HELP HIM......!
DA (DASH)
AH!
BA (WHOOSH)

DOU
(DOOM)
WIDE-AREA MAGIC!?
OH NO!
!?
!
ZAN
(SLASH)

PAKI (CRIK)
PAKIN
PAKI
JIJI (ZZZT)
GYUI (ZOOP)
BA (LEAP)
KIRI—!

BA
(WHAP)
IS HE...?
GUO
(GRAHH)
SU
(SHH)

PASHIIN (KCHANG)
A PERFECT PARRY!
THE ENEMY'S FROZEN!
NOW HE CAN GO ON A COUNTER! BUT...
GAKUN (SLUMP)
...THAT FIGHTING STYLE...
HYU (SWISH)

RAAAAAHH!
DOGAGA (DWAMM)
GYUIN (ZOOP)

フッ
FU (SWISH)
パキャアアン
PAKYAAAN (KRAAACK)
HE'S SO STRONG!

スウッ
SUUU
(SHH)

カシ
KASHIN
(CLINK)
UMM...

THANK YOU FOR PROTECTING US.

NO, IT'S MY FAULT FOR NOT REACTING SOONER.
YOU AREN'T HURT, ARE YOU?
NO, THANKS TO YOU.
JI (STARE)
...SO IT'S NOT HIM, AFTER ALL.
HE DOESN'T USE HIS DUAL BLADES NORMALLY.
AND HIS FIGHTING STYLE IS DIFFER-ENT.

BUT WHAT IF HE STARTED A NEW CHARACTER TO TRY SOMETHING DIFFERENT ...?
HOW WOULD MAKING AN IDENTICAL CHARACTER COUNT AS "DIFFERENT"...?
WE'D RECOGNIZE HIM AT ONCE.
HISO (WHISPER)
UM, HELLO?
OH, SORRY! WE'RE JUST SURPRISED BECAUSE YOU LOOK LIKE A FRIEND OF OURS.
AT FIRST, I THOUGHT KIRITO MIGHT BE BACK TO HIS OLD WAYS OF PUSHING THE LIMITS...
I'M RELIEVED IT WASN'T TRUE.
KIRITO...? YOU KNOW THE GREAT KIRITO-SAMA?
A-ARE YOU...SAO SURVIVORS?
Y-YOU TOO!?
SO YOU DRESSED UP LIKE THAT ON PURPOSE?
LET'S TALK AS WE GO.
ER, ACTUALLY, IT WASN'T INTENTIONAL ...

WHEN I LEARNED THAT THE NEW AINCRAD WAS BEING UNVEILED...
...I BUILT A CHARACTER IN ALO.
I SET THE APPEARANCE VALUES TO RANDOM, AND IT JUST HAPPENED TO GIVE ME THIS LOOK.

JUST LIKE THE HERO KIRITO-SAMA...
...WHO FREED US ALL FROM SAO!

I WAS PERSONALLY INFATUATED WITH HIS POWER AND ABILITY.
SO IT KIND OF FELT LIKE FATE OR SOME-THING.
Then I went and got the same equip-ment...
OH, I SEE NOW.

WELL, COLOR ME SHOCKED.
WE'RE NOT THE ONLY SAO SURVIVORS IN ALO AFTER ALL...
IS IT THAT RARE?
WELL, OF COURSE.
SAO WAS A LITERAL GAME OF DEATH.
ALMOST EVERYONE WHO WAS IN THERE WISHES THEY COULD FORGET THE MEMORIES.
WE MIGHT BE THE CRAZY ONES FOR GOING THROUGH THAT AND STILL WANTING TO PLAY ANOTHER VRMMO.

EVEN I MIGHT NOT HAVE DONE THIS...
...IF IT WEREN'T FOR THOSE MEMORIES...
I... SUPPOSE SO...

BUT...

...I NEVER EXPECTED TO MEET PEOPLE WHO KNOW KIRITO-SAMA HERE.

WE'RE JUST AS SURPRISED AS YOU.
TO (TMP)
TO

BY THE WAY, HOW DO YOU KNOW HIM—

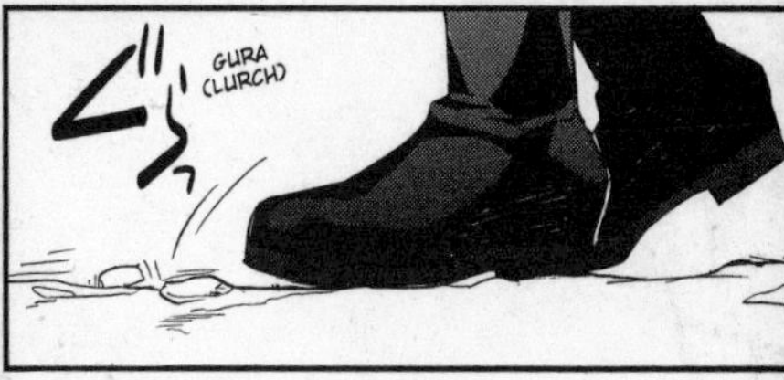
GURA (LURCH)

?
DID YOU FEEL THE GROUND SHAKE?
?
I SURE DID ...

PI
(PWEE)
HUH?
THAT'S RIGHT...
GURA
(LURCH)
GOGO
(GRUNK)
GARA
(KSHUNK)
AAH!
SILICA!
LOOK OUT!!
BA
(LEAP)
DOSA
(THUMP)

Oww... Sorry you had to jump in and help me aga...
ZUZUN (ZDUMM)
EEEK!
GURA (FLOP)
ARE YOU OKAY?
STAY STILL FOR A MOMENT.
PON (PAT)
TH-THANK Y...
AH!

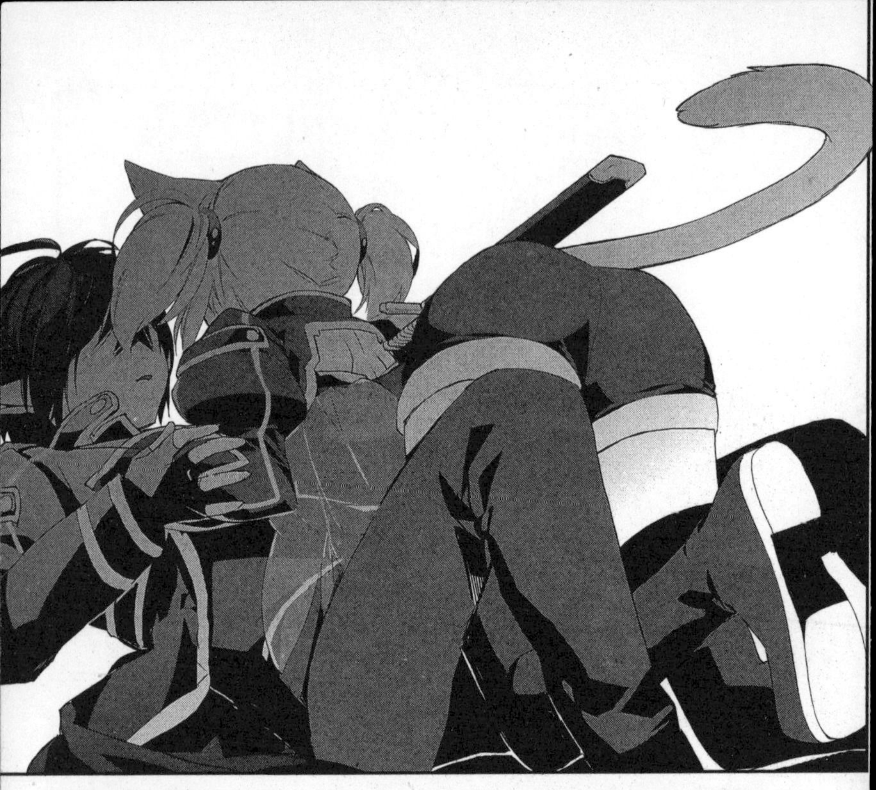

!!?
MEEP

HYAAAAAAA!
GABAA (CLURCH)
I'M SORRY, KIRITO-SA... I MEAN, NOT-KIRITO-SAN!
SILICA, YOU OKAY !?

!?
OH MY, SILICA.
AREN'T WE FORWARD?
MWA HA.
OOOH.
EEEK! IT'S N-N-NOT LIKE THAT! IT JUST HAPPENED WHEN I SLIPPED!

HA-HA, SORRY. I GET IT. JUST CALM DOWN.
FIRST GET OFF.
I'M SORRY! I'M SORRY!
OTHERWISE THE HARASSMENT WARNINGS WILL NEVER STOP.
HUH?

AAAAAA!
THERE'S...NO HARASSMENT WARNING?
HUH?

HARASS-MENT WARNING?
...OH, I THINK I SEE THE CONFUSION.

I MIGHT HAVE DRESSED MY AVATAR UP TO LOOK LIKE KIRITO-SAMA...
SU- (SHH)
スッ
...BUT I'M ACTUALLY A ***WOMAN.***

SHE'S A GIRL!?

SPEAKING OF WHICH, I HAVEN'T INTRO-DUCED MYSELF YET.
WELL, MY NAME IS KURO.
IT STANDS FOR "BLACK," AS IN THE BLACK SWORDSMAN.
SORRY TO CONFUSE YOU, BUT I AM A GIRL.

I'M SILICA.
LISBETH, BUT YOU CAN JUST CALL ME LIZ.
AND I'M LEAFA. NICE TO MEET YOU.

THAT WAS SUCH A SHOCK, I SWEAR.
I'M SORRY— I WASN'T EVEN THINKING ABOUT THAT.
I TEND NOT TO ACT AS FEMININE HERE, GIVEN HOW I LOOK...

UM, I'M NOT CRITICIZING YOU OR ANY-THING!
I MEAN, YOU DID HELP ME!
WA
WA
WA
LET'S CHANGE THE TOPIC.
YOU'RE VERY STRONG THOUGH, KURO-SAN.
I CAN'T BELIEVE YOU BEAT THAT HUGE MONSTER ALL ON YOUR OWN.
AND WITH TWO SWORDS!

IT WASN'T THAT SPECIAL.
I JUST BARELY BEAT IT.
SURA (SLIDE)
PLUS I'M ONLY DOING THE DUAL BLADES THING OUT OF MY RESPECT FOR KIRITO-SAMA.

THE LEFT SWORD IS STRICTLY FOR PARRYING.
MY ACTUAL ATTACKS ARE ALL JUST COPYING THE SINGLE-HANDED SWORD SKILLS I USED BACK IN SAO.

SO THIS DUAL BLADES THING IS JUST FOR SHOW. MY "STRENGTH" IS AN ILLUSION.

WOULDN'T THAT APPLY TO EVERY-ONE?
KIRITO HAD THE DUAL BLADES SKILL IN SAO...
...BUT THAT SKILL DOESN'T EVEN EXIST IN ALO YET.

STILL.
I BET IF IT WAS HIM, HE'D HAVE DESTROYED THAT MONSTER WITHOUT A SWEAT.

I WANT TO BE MUCH STRONGER!
JUST LIKE HIM...
STRONG ENOUGH TO PROTECT EVERYTHING ALL ON MY OWN!
I WISH... I HAD BEEN...

KURO-SA...

パタタ
PATATA (FLAP FLAP)
?
WHAT IS IT?

ACK!
DON (THUMP)
ドン

KURO-SAN?

OH.

THE ANGEL'S ROSE PAVILION...
WHAT COULD HAVE HAPPENED?

OH, NO... THE POOR ROSES.
SEEMS LIKE IT'S BEEN ATTACKED...
AND...
...BY A GIANT.
AH!
I GUESS WHEN IT GOT CONVERTED TO ALO, THEY ADDED SOME GIANTS TO THE MIX TO FIT THE SCANDINAVIAN THEME.
COULD THAT BE WHAT THE RUMBLING WAS EARLIER...?
A BIT OF FORE-SHADOWING TO THE ATTACK.

WELL, THIS IS TURNING INTO QUITE THE ORDEAL.
I'M REMEMBERING THE OLD DAYS, WHEN THE ANGEL WAS FIDGETING AND WAITING FOR US TO RETURN.
"I... I WASN'T WORRIED ABOUT YOU OR ANYTHING, JUST SO YOU KNOW!"
HMPH!
SEEMS LIKE THE TSUNDERE-ANGEL IS NOW JUST PLAIN HEART-WARMING.
HA-HA, YOU SOUND JUST LIKE HER.
HMPH!
SPEAKING OF WHICH, WHERE IS THAT TSUNDERE-ANGEL...?
URK?
...A FEATHER?
IT APPEARS TO BE A MANIPULABLE OBJECT.
SHALL I?
GO AHEAD.
CHIRIIN (TINK)
PAAA (GLOW)

ABOUT DAMN TIME YOU RETURNED!

BUT YOU'VE RUN OVER THE TIME LIMIT.
THE TRIAL WAS A FAILURE. TOO BAD.
パタタ
PATATA (FLAP)
I HAVE NO RING FOR YOU.
NOW GET LOST!

AND DON'T YOU DARE THINK OF COMING AFTER ME...
BUTSUN (CLICK)
SHE VAN-ISHED...
WHAT WAS THAT...?
HEE HEE!
LIZ-SAN?
A RANSACKED ROSE GARDEN, A KIDNAPPED ANGEL, AND AN INSULT MEANT TO KEEP US AWAY...

THINGS ARE REALLY HEATING UP IN THIS QUEST. I LIKE IT!
HEH HEH HEH...
MAYBE IT'S NOT JUST OUR BONDS TO EACH OTHER, BUT OUR BONDS TO THE ANGEL THAT ARE BEING TESTED?
THIS IS GETTING KINDA FUN.
SEEMS LIKE LIZ-SAN IS REALLY EXCITED ABOUT THIS.
I DON'T HAVE A PROBLEM WITH IT EITHER.
ME TOO
NOW, WE OUGHT TO HEAD...

...IN THE DIRECTION OF THE GIANT'S FOOT-STEPS.

LET'S RESCUE OUR TSUNDERE-ANGEL AND MAKE HER ALL SAPPY FOR US!
RIGHT!
DON'T WORRY, WE'RE RIGHT ON YOUR HEELS.
TSUN (POKE)
OH, RIGHT.
THIS MUST BE FATE AT WORK!
KURO-SAN, WILL YOU JOIN—
I'M SORRY, BUT...

I'M GOING...
...TO HANDLE THIS ALONE.

HUH?

Wh-what's the matter, Kuro-san?
Did we do something wrong?

NO, NO.
I MEAN, UM...
I GOT A LITTLE CARRIED AWAY WHEN I LEARNED THAT YOU KNOW KIRITO-SAMA...
...BUT I DO NOT HAVE ANY INTENTION OF FORMING A PARTY IN THIS GAME.
SO WE MUST SAY GOOD-BYE HERE.

OH, NO... BUT IT'S AN ONLINE GAME AND EVERY-THING.

I UNDER-STAND WHAT YOU MEAN.
BUT I MADE THIS DECISION FOR MYSELF.

BUT...

...THERE MIGHT BE MONSTERS FAR DEADLIER THAN THE ONE YOU ALREADY FOUGHT WAITING AHEAD!
IT'S DANGEROUS TO GO ALONE!

DANGER-OUS?
HA HA.

YOU KNOW THAT'S NOT TRUE, DON'T YOU, SILICA?

IT'S ALL "JUST A GAME" AGAIN.
DYING HERE...
...DOESN'T MEAN DYING FOR REAL.

IT WAS FUN TALKING TO ALL OF YOU.
BUT NOW, I MUST BE OFF.
SU (SWISH)
スッ
IF YOU WAIT A BIT, THE QUEST WILL BE RESET, SO YOU CAN CONTINUE ON YOUR OWN.
SAWA (SWOOSH)
Um...
FUWA (FWUF)

I KNOW IT'S WORRYING...
...BUT IT WAS KURO-SAN WHO BEAT THAT MID-BOSS EARLIER.
WE CAN'T STOP HER.

YES...I KNOW.

I WONDER...
...IF SHE LOST SOMEONE IMPORTANT TO HER TOO...
...IN SAO.

... SILICA ...
—
GYU (SQUEEZE)
...SHALL WE FOLLOW HER?
HUH?

LIZ-SAN, LEAFA-SAN...
...WE SHOULD GO AFTER HER.
BUT...
...THERE'S NO GUARANTEE WE'LL BE ANY HELP IF WE DO CATCH UP...
BUT WE HAVEN'T DONE A THING IN THE FIRST PLACE!
SILICA ...
Ah!
S-sorry...

IF SHE REALLY WANTED TO BE ALONE, I WOULDN'T BOTHER HER.
BUT...

...YOU DON'T SMILE LIKE THAT IF YOU WANT TO BE LEFT ALONE.

BUT SHE MUST BE BEARING SOME BURDEN THAT CAUSES HER TO MAKE THAT CHOICE.
I DON'T THINK IT'S SHEER COINCIDENCE THAT SHE LOOKS SO MUCH LIKE KIRITO-SAN.
IN WHICH CASE ...

...I WANT TO BE A SOURCE OF STRENGTH FOR HER.
JUST LIKE KIRITO-SAN WAS WHEN HE REACHED OUT TO ME.

MAYBE I'M JUST BEING NOSY WHEN I SHOULDN'T...
...BUT DON'T YOU AGREE THERE ARE THINGS THAT CAN'T BE SOLVED ALONE?
SO IF THERE'S SOMETHING I CAN DO FOR HER, I WANT TO DO IT.
WE ONLY JUST MET HER.
WOULDN'T IT BE A SHAME IF WE HAD TO JUST SAY GOOD-BYE WITHOUT KNOWING WHY?
And besides...
...I know she's a different person entirely, and this might be an extremely private and personal reason to bother her, but...

COULD YOU REALLY IGNORE...
...A KIRITO-SAN LIKE THAT?
GYU (SQUEEZE)
!!
DID YOU JUST GO THERE?
OH, I WENT THERE.
EVEN AFTER WE KNEW IT WASN'T HIM, HE'S A BIG PART OF THE REASON.
SOME-TIMES I CAN'T STAND THAT GUY!
OH, GEEZ...

LET'S GO.
TA (TEK)
NO REGRETS !!

SWORD ART ONLINE
GIRLS' OPS

I FEEL SO... INADE-QUATE!!
SILICA
LEAFA'S CLOTHES

STAGE.3

BACK IN SAO, I COULDN'T TRUST ANYONE ELSE.

BUT...

IT'S AN ITEM THAT SYMBOLIZES THE BOND BETWEEN TWO PEOPLE!
IT WAS ACTUALLY PRETTY HARD TO GET!
YOU'RE SUPPOSED TO HAVE TWO AND EXCHANGE THEM...
...BUT FOR NOW, IT'S JUST A ONE-WAY THING. SO THIS GOES FROM ME TO YOU.

...EVEN THEN, SHE REACHED OUT FOR ME.

I JUST HOPE...

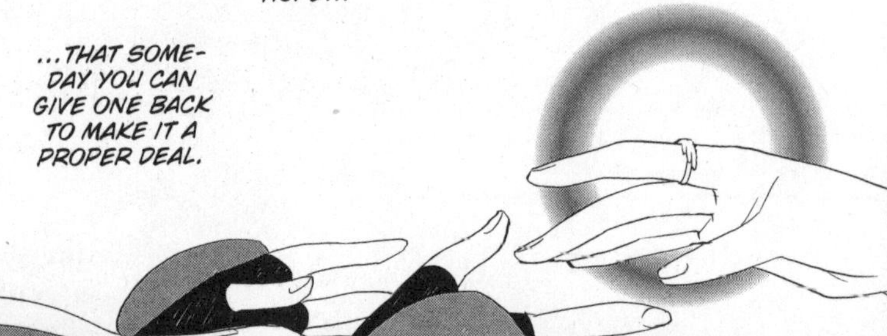

...THAT SOMEDAY YOU CAN GIVE ONE BACK TO MAKE IT A PROPER DEAL.

SO I JUST WANT...

..TO FULFILL THAT PROMISE...

DO YOU SUPPOSE KURO-SAN'S ALL RIGHT?
I THINK SHE'S FINE.
YOU SAW HOW TOUGH SHE WAS AGAINST THAT BOSS EARLIER.
IN BATTLE TERMS, ISN'T IT YOU WHO'D BE IN MORE DANGER, SILICA?
Th-that's not true!
Um...I think...
OH, I'M JUST KIDDING! YOU'RE ALWAYS A HUGE HELP, SILICA.
ポン
PON (PAT)
SO...
EVERYONE READY?
NOT JUST FOR THE BATTLE AHEAD.
YES!

I MEAN FOR HOW SHE MIGHT REACT...
...AFTER WARNING US NOT TO COME.

I'M READY!

GOOD ANSWER.

THEN, LET'S GO!
GII (CREAK)

WHOA, WHAT IS THIS!?
SLIMES!?
THEY'RE EVERY-WHERE!!
UZOZOZO (SQUIRM)
PI (BEEP)
ARE YOU SUPPOSED TO SURVIVE THROUGH THE COUNTDOWN?
THERE'S NO WAY A SOLO PLAYER CAN HANDLE THIS......!
UZO (OOZE)
UZO

ZAN
(SLICE)

BA
(WHOOSH)
YOU GUYS!
WHY DID YOU COME HERE!?

KURO-SAN!
TA
(TEK)

ZA
(SLASH)

TO (THUD)

I TOLD YOU, I WANT TO DO THIS ALO...
I'M SORRY!

I HEARD WHAT YOU SAID, AND I UNDERSTAND.
BUT EVEN SO, I COULDN'T LET YOU GO LIKE THAT.
IF YOU'VE GOT SOME-THING HEAVY ON YOUR MIND...I WANT TO HELP.
THE REASON YOU LOOK SO MUCH LIKE KIRITO-SAN IS SO THAT WE CAN HELP YOU, AS HIS FRIENDS!

SILICA, THAT'S NONE OF YOUR...
AH!
EEEEW!

WHAT'S WITH THESE SLIMES!?
THEY SPIT ACID!? IT'S RUINING MY ARMOR!
JU (FZZ)
じゅっ
AND THE DAMAGE IS REALLY HIGH!
ブジュル
BUJURU (SPLURP)
GYUN (ZOOP)
ギュ

UZOZO... (SQUIRM)
ウゾゾゾ
LIZ-SAN!
ZAN (SLASH)
!?
KURO-SAN!
THANKS!
ZA (ZSHH)

SILICA, SWING AROUND THE LEFT, AND GATHER THE ENEMIES UP.
I'LL HACK AWAY FROM THE FRONT.
KURO-SAN!
UZOZOZOZO (SQUIRM)
I'M NOT SAYING WE SHOULD WORK TOGETHER.
WE'RE JUST HANDLING THIS FLOOR'S BATTLE SIMULTANEOUSLY.
WE'LL START FROM THERE.
...OKAY!

TA (TEK)

SILICA...
...YOU'RE JUST AS NOSY AND KINDHEARTED AS SHE WAS.
AND THIS TIME...
SU (SWISH)

GU (CLENCH)
I'LL KEEP YOU ALIVE!
DA (STOMP)
SEIYA!
ZAN (SLASH)
GA (WHAK)
GA
GA
GA
GA

SILICA!

WE'RE GOING TO KNOCK OUT THE SLIMES FIRST.
THEN WE CAN TALK.

OKAY, SOUNDS GOOD.
THE PROBLEM WITH THESE SLIMES IS...

UZOZO (SQUIRM)
...THEY'RE NOT HARD TO BEAT...
...BUT THERE ARE TOO MANY TO HANDLE SAFELY.
GUGU (HRRG)

ARRGH! THESE ARMOR-MELTING ATTACKS ARE TERRIBLE! THE GMs MUST BE DEMONS!
ボロッ
BORO (RAGGED)
PLUS THIS DAMAGE IS REALLY STARTING TO ADD UP!
ボロッ
BORO

BORO
I-I'M JUST GLAD THE REAL KIRITO-SAN ISN'T HERE TO SEE THIS!
BA (WHOOSH)
JUUU (FZZ)
BASHA (SPLAT)
ZAN (SLASH)

BORO
(RAGGED)
KURO......!
KURO-SAN'S TAKEN THE MOST DAMAGE OF ANYONE...
...BECAUSE SHE'S BEEN SO BUSY COVERING FOR US.
BO
(FWOOM)
ZURUU...
(SLURP)
POTORI
(PLOP)
SUSU
(SLIDE)
WE'VE GOT TO FINISH THIS CHALLENGE QUICK, OR WE WON'T LAST!

THAT'S THE LAST ONE!
BECHORI (SLURM)
べちょり
NOW AS LONG AS WE CAN WIPE OUT THE SLIMES THAT ARE SLIDING AROUND...!
UM, KURO-SAN!?
DA (DASH)
GUWA (GRAH)
THIS IS THE END!

YOU CAN'T DO THIS, KURO-SAN!
DON'T RUSH AHEAD...
ZUGAGAGA (THWABAAM)
JUST THREE LEFT!

GA (WHAKK)

I... DIDN'T REACH THEM!?

ZO (SHIVER)
GUGUGU (HRRGG)
DAMN, NOW I'M FROZEN AFTER USING THAT HEAVY ATTACK...!

WATCH OUT!

SAA
(SWISH)

BUJURU
(SPLOOP)
ブジュル

JUO (FZSHH)
HYAA!!
DO (THUMP)
SHUUU... (HSSS)

SILICA!!
AH!
DA (LEAP)
DA
DO (THWAM)
ZAN (SLICE)

BA
(WHOOSH)
ばっ

THAT WAS...
...THE LAST ONE!

...!
WHOA!
KUWAN (SWIRL)
KUWAN
TAKING THOSE THREE HITS REALLY MADE MY HEAD SPIN!
silica
AND MY HP IS NEARLY GONE!
GOOD THING I WAS ABLE TO WITH-STAND IT FOR YOU.
YIPES!
OOPS.
SORRY ABOUT BUMPING INTO YOU LIKE THAT, KURO-SAN...
KURU (SPIN)
PORO (DRIP)

KURO...
WHY!?
WHY DID YOU PROTECT ME!?
WHY!?
WHAT'S THE POINT OF DOING THAT...
...IF YOU NEVER COME BACK!?

KARAN
(CLANG)
I DON'T EVER WANT TO GO THROUGH THAT AGAIN...!
DON'T LEAVE ME ALL ALONE...
GYU
(SQUEEZE)
ぎゅっ

...ROSSA!
WHY...?

I KNEW IT. SHE DID LOSE SOMEONE CLOSE TO HER...
GATA (RATTLE)
GATA
GATA

AND THAT'S WHY SHE DOES IT ALL ALONE...

GYU (SQUEEZE)
CALM DOWN, KURO-SAN.
I'M JUST FINE.

I'M RIGHT HERE.

TA (TEK)
SILICA, KURO, YOU OKAY?
I'M ALL RIGHT.
BUT KURO-SAN...
WHAT HAPPENED TO HER?
I DON'T KNOW FOR CERTAIN...
...BUT PERHAPS WE SHOULD GIVE UP ON THIS QUEST FOR NOW AND HEAD BACK TO TOWN FOR A BIT.
GOOD IDEA. IN THAT CASE...
OH!
WAIT!
THE COUNT-DOWN'S STILL RUN-NING...
KACHIRI (CLIK)

BIKYA (RIIIP)
AAAAH!!
BISHII (CRAKK)
BIKI (CRIK)
WHAT'S GOING ON!?
BIKI
BIKI
BIKI

ビキ。。
BIKI
THE ROOM... SHIFTED?
WELCOME TO MY CHAMBER.
IS THIS WHAT I THINK —!?

WAS IT JUST A TELEPORTER TO THE BOSS CHAMBER ......!?

NOW, ANGEL, WATCH AS THE BONDS YOU HELD SO DEAR CRUMBLE INTO DUST!!

I REALLY DO FEEL LIKE ONII-CHAN!
EEEK!
LEAFA
KURO'S CLOTHES

STAGE.4
A FORCED TELEPORT TO THE BOSS CHAMBER!?

HOW CAN THEY THROW US INTO A BOSS FIGHT...
Lisbeth
Leafa
...IN OUR CURRENT CONDITION!?
silica

THERE'S NO ESCAPE FROM THIS PLACE!
BA (WHOOSH)
FIRST WE NEED HEALING!
THÚ FYLLA HEILAGR...
PO (POP)
PO
PO
GUWA (GWOOSH)

DO
(BOOM)
AAAAH!

...IT INTER-
RUPTED MY
CAST...!
ぱしゅ
PASHU
(SHWUP)

THERE'S
NO WAY
FOR US TO
RECOVER.
WE'RE
ALL...

OOOO (OHHH)

BUO (WHOOSH)
...ABOUT TO GET WIPED OUT...

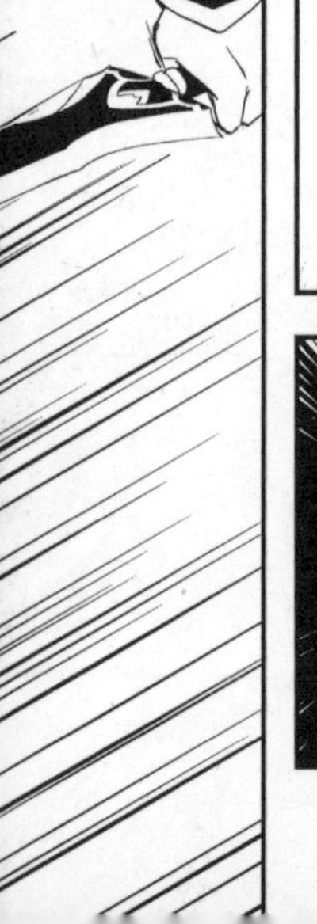

GYU (SQUEEZE)
WE CAN'T START OVER FROM TOWN, NOT AFTER WE CAME THIS FAR...

GI
(CHING)
GIGI
(RRGH)
GYAIN
(SHYANG)

ZUZAA (SLIDE)
KURO-SAN!
KURO!
YOU CAN'T...
DON'T DIE ON ME...
GUGU (HRRG)
I'M TIRED OF PEOPLE DISAPPEARING ...

I CAN'T TAKE IT ANY-MORE!!
...KURO!?

THERE IS NO DEATH IN THIS WORLD.
JUST A MOMENT EARLIER...
...KURO-SAN SEEMED CONFUSED. WHEN I STEPPED IN TO PROTECT HER, SHE WAS SEEING SOMEONE ELSE...
BUT IF WE DON'T DO SOME-THING...

...KURO-SAN'S HEART ITSELF WILL WITHER AND DIE...!
AH!
ZUN (ZMM)

PAN (SMACK)
パン

I'LL DRAW THE ENEMY AWAY.
LEAFA, YOU FOCUS ON HEALING.
UM, OKAY!

SILICA, TAKE CARE OF KURO.
PON (PAT)
ぽん

SU (SWISH)
すっ

SHOW ME YOU HAVE WHAT IT TAKES TO OWN UP TO YOUR CHOICE TO GO AFTER HER!
BI (JAB)

I WILL!
DA (DSHH)
THŪ FYLLA...
...HEI-LAGR...
POU (GLOW)
...AUSTR...

BA (SMACK)
...BROTT SVALR BANI!

KYUWA (TWINKLE)
THANKS, LEAFA.
GUWA (WHOOSH)

DON
(BOOM)
TAN
(LEAP)
I'VE GOT...
...MY MOMENTS TOO, Y'KNOW!
GO
(WHAM)
HIYAAAH!!

GURA (WOBBLE)
GUOO (GRAHH)
SHUUU (FSHHH)
...SVALR BANI!
NICE SHOT, LIZ-SAN!
PAAA (GLOW)
KYUWA (TWINKLE)
NO SWEAT!
I'M OVER HERE, MONSTER!
ZUN (ZMM)
ZUN

IT'S TIMES LIKE THIS...
...THAT LIZ-SAN REALLY SHINES.
KYURURU...

POFUN (POOF)
ポフン
PINA!
THANKS FOR THE HEALING.
KYU!

PECHIN (SMACK)
ぺちん
OKAY!

KURO-SAN!
SILICA!
TA (TEK)
タッ
YOU NEED TO GET AWAY FROM HERE!
I'LL HANDLE HIM...
GAKU (SLUMP)
ガクッ
DAMN... WHY CAN'T I MOVE...? WHY NOW?
WHEN I JUST WANT TO PROTECT YOU.
KATA (SHIVER)
KATA
KATA
カタカタカタ

WHEN I WANT TO MAKE SURE I DON'T LOSE YOU AGAIN!
KURO-SAN, CALM DOWN.
I NEED STRENGTH ...

STRENGTH LIKE KIRITO THE HERO...
ENOUGH STRENGTH TO PROTECT EVERY SINGLE THING ON MY OWN...
GUGU (CLENCH)

...YOU'RE WRONG.

THE HERO KIRITO THAT YOU WORSHIP, THE ONE WHO SAVED SAO, WASN'T ALONE.

KIRITO-SAN SAID...
...THAT IT WAS EVERYONE WHO LIVED THROUGH SAO THAT SUCCEEDED IN FREEING IT.

THOSE ON THE LOWER AND MIDDLE FLOORS WHO SUPPORTED US.

THOSE ON THE FRONT LINES WHO FOUGHT ALONGSIDE US.

THOSE PRECIOUS SOULS...
...AT OUR SIDE.
IT WAS THROUGH A GREAT MANY PEOPLE COMING TOGETHER THAT WE ACHIEVED OUR GOAL.
THAT'S WHAT HE'S LIKE.

AND IT'S WHY WE'RE ABLE...
...TO FIGHT AT HIS SIDE.

HE'S NOT ALONE.
WE WON'T LET HIM BE.

AND THE SAME GOES FOR YOU!

POPON (PING)
ポポーン
CHIRIN (JINGLE)
チリーン
PON (BING)
ポーン

A...party request...?
Will you join the party?
YES.
I WANT KURO-SAN TO CHOOSE TO BE WITH US OF HER OWN FREE WILL...

LET'S FIGHT TOGETHER!

...But...
PWEE!
BASA (FLAP)
HUH? PINA...
MOFUUN (PWOOF)
HYEEP!

KIRA (SPARKLE)
KIRA

AAAAH!
PINA, HOW COULD YOU!?
SHE'S NOT IN THE PARTY YET!
PWEE!
AWA
WA
KURO-SAN, I'M SO SORRY ABOUT THAT!
WA WA WA WA WA WA WA WA
GASHII (SNATCH)
KYU-RURU.
BUT SHE WAS ALL BEATEN UP...
UH, DON'T WORRY— IT'S JUST HEALING BREATH!
KYUU... YOU OKAY?
PFFT!

HA HA HA HA!
YOU'RE SO FUNNY, SILICA...

K... KURO-SAN!
WELL, THAT WAS QUITE A SURPRISE.
YORO (WOBBLE)
よろ
AAAAAH!
S-SORRY!
BUT...

I SUPPOSE TAMED MONSTERS SOMETIMES ACT ON THEIR OWN, EVEN WITHOUT ORDERS.
ER, NO.
THAT'S NOT HOW IT'S SUPPOSED TO WORK...

OH.
WHAT A STRANGE LITTLE CREATURE WITH A MIND OF ITS OWN. ALMOST AS THOUGH IT'S NOT DIGITAL DATA.
KRU-RU-RU!
PERHAPS IN YOUR HEAD, I'M ALREADY A MEMBER OF THE GROUP.
PINA...

SIGH...

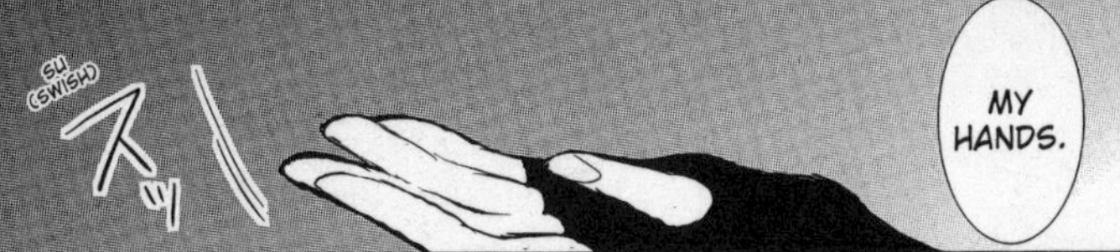
MY HANDS.
SU (SWISH)

THEY'RE STILL SHAKING.
FURU (SHAKE)
FURU
I'M STILL TERRIFIED BY THE THOUGHT...
...OF SOME-ONE DISAP-PEAR-ING.

DON'T WORRY.
WE'LL NEVER JUST UP AND VANISH!
PWEE!

SU (SHH)
BASA (FLAP)
PON (BING)
Will you join the party?

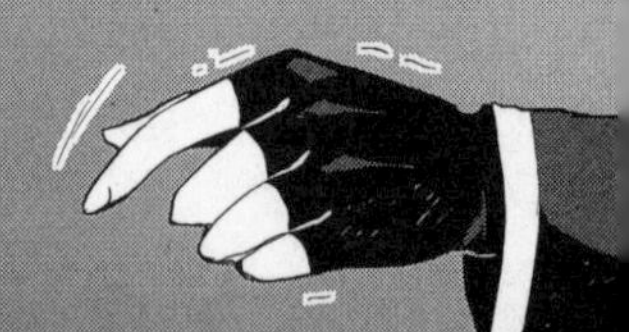

GYU
(SQUEEZE)
ぎゅっ
LET'S BEAT THIS QUEST TOGETHER!

AS A TEAM!

IT FEELS ODD TO DRESS IN WOMEN'S CLOTHES WITH THIS AVATAR...
...BUT IT DOES LOOK GOOD ON ME.
KURO
LISBETH'S CLOTHES

STAGE. 5
GYANGIGIN (KCHAANG)
GAGA (GRRG)
YOU SHARE NO SPECIAL BOND.
BUO (WHOOSH)
BA (LEAP)
GAGA (WHAM)
HA (GASP)

BOW BEFORE MY OVER-WHELMING MIGHT!!

EEYAA!!

...!
CHIRIN (TINKLE)
TAN (TMP)

CHIRIN

GOKU (GULP)
KYUWA (WHOOSH)

PAKIN (CRACKLE)
THERE GOES MY LAST POTION.
AND LEAFA-SAN'S MANA POINTS ARE ABOUT TO RUN OUT.
PAAA (GLOW)
BUT...

...THE BOSS STILL HAS AN ENTIRE HP GAUGE LEFT!
IT SURE WAS ROUGH OF THEM TO DUMP US STRAIGHT INTO THE BOSS FIGHT AFTER THE SLIMES.
チリン
CHIRIN (TINKLE)
ふわっ
FUWA (FWUFF)
ON TOP OF THAT...
LIZ-SAN?
ゴクッ
GOKU (GULP)

HIS CHEST IS THE SPOT THAT TAKES THE MOST DAMAGE...
...BUT HE'S CONVENIENTLY DRAPED THE TSUNDERE-ANGEL RIGHT IN THE WAY...!
IT'S HARD NOT TO HIT HER...
JUST WHAT WE NEED—A CLASSIC DAMSEL IN DISTRESS.
HA-HA, GOOD POINT...
ゴクッ
GOKU (GULP)

SHALL WE GO AHEAD AND ATTACK, KNOWING SHE WON'T BE HAPPY ABOUT THAT?

パキン
PAKIN (CRAK)

NO WAY.
HEH HEH!

ぱっ
BA (LEAP)
IF SHE ACTS DIFFERENTLY WHEN YOU SPARE HER, I'D RATHER HOLD BACK AND SEE WHAT OUR TSUNDERE-ANGEL DOES!
GOOD POINT—I'D LIKE TO SEE THAT!
HYU (SWISH)
ZUGAGAGA (ZDOOM)
SEIYA!
GUN (ZMMF)

LEAFA-
SAN!
AH!
BA
(LEAP)
SWITCH
OUT!
KURO!
GYU
(CLENCH)
I'LL
EXECUTE
A PERFECT
PARRY...
...AND
FINISH
WITH A
BLOW!
HYUO
(SWISH)

OH NO...
MY TIMING WAS OFF!
GYARIWWE (KCHING)
GOU (WHOOSH)
GA (WHAM)
LEAFA-SAN!?

GIGIN (KTINNG)
...!

WHEW!
THAT WAS A CLOSE ONE!
I'm sorry.
I screwed up the parry, and you had to cover for me...

NO WOR-RIES!
THANKS FOR TRYING TO HELP, THOUGH!

BA (WHOOSH)

GU (CLUTCH)

DAMN! I ONLY WANT TO HELP...
...BUT MY HANDS WON'T STOP SHAKING...
AND RIGHT AFTER THEY WELCOMED ME WITH OPEN ARMS...!
LET THE BOLTS OF LIGHTNING SPRAY!
BAJI (BZZAP)
BAJI
AH!
OH NO...!

AH!
WE'VE GOT TO DODGE THE BOLTS!
HERE COMES THE AREA ATTACK!
I KNOW!
BACHII (ZZAP)
BACHI
ZUGAN (KABOOM)
ZUGAN

DODODODO
(DOOOM)
IT'S A HUGE WIDE-AREA BLAST!
ACK!
BACHII
(BZAP)
DO
(DOOOM)
IT MIGHT BE DIFFICULT TO AVOID...
DON
(BOOOM)
DON
DONN

...BUT THAT JUST MEANS IT'LL TAKE HIM LONGER...
...TO RECOVER AFTER USING IT!!
PITA (FREEZE)
YAAAAAAH!
GAGA (WHAM)
GAGA

GA (WHAK)
GA
GA
DA (LEAP)
GOT A LATE JUMP!
GA
GA
GA
GA
HYU (SWISH)
IF WE CAN JUST...
...GET HIM ALL THE WAY DOWN—!

GAN (WHAK)
GIN (GLINT)
GUWA (RAHH)
HUH!?
WHY!? HE SHOULD HAVE HAD A LONGER COOLDOWN PERIOD!

I PRAISE YOU FOR PUSHING ME TO MY LIMIT. HOW-EVER...
GYUOO (ZWOOSH)
AH!
IT MUST BE SET TO REDUCE THE INTERVAL WHEN HIS HEALTH GETS LOW!

AT THIS RATE, WE WON'T BE ABLE TO EVADE OR FIND COVER IN TIME!
...THIS IS THE END FOR YOU, LITTLE WINGED INSECTS!!
ZUGAGAGA (ZDOOM)
AAAAH!!!

ZUZAA (SLIDE)
HIOO (CHYOOSH)

GAGAGA (BABABAM)
NOT SO FAST!
GA (BAM)
LIZ-SAN!

HE TOOK DOWN ALL MY HP, EVEN WITH MY GUARD UP!
GYUN (ZOOP)
AND...
Lisbeth

...HIS COMBO'S NOT STOPPING!
PAA (GLOW)
GUO (WHOOSH)
PACHI (BLINK)
AH!
STOP, LIZ-SAN! YOU CAN'T HOLD OUT!
YOU'VE GOT TO RUN FOR IT!
HEE HEE.

IT'S ALL RIGHT!

BASAA (FLAP)
ばさぁ
WHAT ARE YOU DOING? IF YOU'RE GOING TO COME ALL THE WAY TO RESCUE ME, DO IT RIGHT!

KYUWA (SWOOSH)

KIRA
IS THIS...
...THE ANGEL'S HEALING MAGIC!?
KIRA (SPARKLE)

SURE, IT LOOKED SCARY, BUT WHENEVER YOU WERE ON THE ROPES, IT WOULD OCCASIONALLY THROW BUFFS ON YOU.
I KNEW IT WAS ACTUALLY THE ANGEL IN DISGUISE RIGHT AWAY.
OH!
EVEN BACK IN SAO, SHE GAVE US HELP WHEN SHE WAS SPARKLING WITH HER EYES OPEN!
SOME PEOPLE JUST DON'T KNOW HOW TO SAY THANKS NORMALLY!

GYUO (WHOOSH)
BUT NOW...
GAGAGAN (GSHAMM)
...WE CAN HOLD OUT!
Lisbeth
PITA (FREEZE)

...WHY?

YOU DON'T REALLY DIE IN THIS GAME WORLD.

THEY MUST HAVE RESURRECTION ITEMS ON HAND.

SO WHY ARE THEY GOING THROUGH WITH THIS RECKLESS PLAN...

...JUST FOR THE SAKE...

...OF MY WEAK MIND AND HEART...?

I WANT TO FIGHT...
I WANT TO FIGHT WITH THEM!
GUWA (GRAHH)

HERE COMES THE NEXT ATTACK! LIZ-SAN, STEP AWAY...
EVERY-ONE BACK!
HUH?
KURO ...!?
I'M GOING TO STOP HIM!
BA (WHOOSH)
MAYBE THEY WON'T LET ME HANDLE THIS, KNOWING WHAT A WRECK I AM.
JUST LET ME...
BUT...

OKAY.

WE UNDER-STAND!
GOU (DOOOM)
HYU (SWISH)

THE TREMBLING...
...STOPPED.
IT WAS THAT EASY.
NOW...
...I CAN TRUST THEM TO HANDLE THE REST.
I JUST NEED TO DO WHAT I CAN DO.

FOCUS ON THE TIMING OF THE PARRY.
RIGHT ON THAT SINGLE POINT...

...AND PIERCE.

GAKUN
(SLUMP)
ガク

NOW!
YAAAAAAH!
BASA (FLAP)

DO
(BOOM)
GYUN
(ZOOP)

BAKIN (CRUNCH)
IM... POSSIBLE ...
BAKI (CRACK)
BAKI
HOW COULD I BE UNDONE... BY THE BONDS... BETWEEN MERE INSECTS...?
PAKIN (CRAASH)

WE DID IT!
FUWA (PUFF)

BASA (FLAP)
NICE GOING ...
... FAIRIES.

I DON'T RECALL EVER ASKING YOU TO SAVE ME...
HMPH!
...BUT... THANKS.
SHE WAS "TSUN" TO THE END!

I HAVE SEEN YOUR BOND FOR MYSELF.
I SUPPOSE IT WAS WORTH THE TROUBLE OF TAKING THE FORM OF AN ANGEL.
SUUU (SHH)

PAA (GLOW)
FUWA (FLOAT)
MAY YOUR CONNECTION LAST LONG.

I NOW ENHANCE YOUR BONDS...
...WITH THE ANGEL'S BLESSING.
A HOST OF VAL-KYRIES ...?
DOES THIS MEAN SHE'S A GODDESS IN THE FORM OF AN ANGEL?
I SUP-POSE SO.
KINDA FUNNY HOW THEY ADAPTED IT INTO AN ALO QUEST.

KIRA
(SPARKLE)
キラッ

LOOK WHAT WE GOT!
ANGEL'S WHISPER RINGS!
SAWA (WHOOSH)
WELL, THAT QUEST WAS A REAL BUTT-KICKER!
SAWA (WHOOSH)
SAWA
I KNOW...
THE DIFFICULTY WAS SET SUPER-HIGH.
GU (CLENCH)
I HAVE A SUGGESTION.

WHY DON'T THE FOUR OF US EXCHANGE RINGS?

ARE YOU SURE, KURO-SAN?
YOU WERE DOING THIS QUEST ON YOUR OWN TO GET A RING, RIGHT?
YES.

THE REASON I WAS TRYING MY HARDEST TO BEAT THE QUEST...
...WAS TO FULFILL A PROMISE I MADE TO SOMEONE IN SAO BACK WHEN I HAD LOST ALL TRUST IN OTHERS...
SHE GAVE ME ONE OF THESE...
KIRA (SPARKLE)

...AND THEN DIED IN THE ACT OF PROTECTING ME FROM HARM.
THE THING IS...
...SHE WAS SO PUSHY ABOUT DOING GOOD FOR THE SAKE OF OTHERS...
...I FEEL LIKE SHE'D BE HAPPIER...
...KNOWING I USED IT FOR THE SAKE OF FUTURE FRIENDS RATHER THAN ON HER, NOW THAT SHE'S GONE.
THAT'S JUST...
...WHAT ROSSA WAS LIKE.

AH!
B-but I'm not going to force you, of course...

PASHI (SNATCH)
ぱしっ

SU (SHH)
スッ

MAYBE IT WAS ROSSA-SAN...
...WHO HELPED YOU MEET US.

FUWA (PUFF)
SO THAT MEANS IT'S NOT THE FOUR OF US... IT'S FIVE!
SILICA...!
LIZ.
LEAFA.

...ROSSA.

...THANK YOU.
TAKE GOOD CARE OF HER.

THEN I'LL GET KURO'S!
HYOI (ZWIP)
ひょいっ
LIZ-SAN?

AWW!
LOS-ERS, WEEP-ERS!
YOU CAN HAVE MINE, LEAFA.
WELL, I'D BE GLAD TO TAKE IT, BUT STILL...
HEE HEE!
ALL I'VE BEEN DOING IS LEVELING MY SKILLS, SO I DON'T KNOW MUCH ABOUT ALO.
WILL YOU TEACH ME?
OH, REALLY?
IN THAT CASE...
FUWA (FLOAT)
WELCOME TO THE LAND OF THE FAIRIES...
..."ALFHEIM ONLINE"!

COME ENJOY THE GAME WITH US!
I WILL!
TA (LEAP)
OH, RIGHT! I WANT YOU ALL TO KNOW...
MY REAL NAME...

...IS HIYORI KASHIWAZAKA. IT'S A PLEASURE TO MAKE YOUR ACQUAINTANCE.

PI?
KORON
(ROLL)
PINA
+
SILICA'S CLOTHES

STAGE. 6
3rd Period
Girls have
unified P.E.
Report to gym
I HAVE TO SAY...
...THAT WAS A HUGE SURPRISE, THE DAY THAT HIYORI-SAN TRANSFERRED TO OUR SCHOOL.
GAYA (CHATTER)
GAYA
GAYA
I MEAN, TO HEAR SOMEONE SUDDENLY START YELLING YOUR AVATAR NAMES AT SCHOOL...

TA (TEK)
SILICA!
LIZ!
TA
TA
I FINALLY FOUND YOU!

タ―ン
TAN
(HOP)

UM...
ほわ
HOWA (POOF)
...WHO!?

It's kind of shocking when a person you don't know comes up...
...and grabs your hand out of nowhere.
S-SORRY ABOUT THAT.
I JUST REALIZED HOW CLOSELY YOU AND SILI...KEIKO-SAN RESEMBLED YOUR ALO AVATARS, AND I COULDN'T HELP MYSELF...

WEIRDEST OF ALL...
...WAS HOW KURO, WHO LOOKED SO MUCH LIKE KIRITO...
...TURNED OUT TO BE SUCH A FLOOFY GIRL LIKE HER.

A TRUE, REAL...
... SHOCKER ...
FIRST SUGUHA-SAN, NOW THIS...
ド
DON (BOOM)

WERE YOU JUST EYEING WHAT I THINK YOU WERE, KEIKO?
I WASN'T EYEING ANYTHING AT ALL!
ニヤ
NIYA (SMIRK)
ニヤ
NIYA
HMPH!

I WASN'T ABLE TO GO TO SCHOOL RIGHT AFTER RETURNING FROM SAO...
...SO IT'S LESS A TRANSFER THAN JUST THAT I FINALLY GOT IN.
I NEEDED A GOOD PUSH ON THE BACK IN REAL LIFE.

THANK YOU.

PON (PAT)
HURRY UP GETTING CHANGED, AND LET'S GO.

OKAY.
KYU (ZIP)
キュッ
ポーン
PONN (BOING)
I WONDER WHAT I SHOULD WEAR...
WHAT? YOU GOT A DATE?
TON (BOP)
トン
NO, NOT REAL CLOTHES. I'M TALKING ABOUT MY ARMOR IN ALO.
EVER SINCE THE SLIMES IN THAT "ANGEL'S WHISPER RING" QUEST MELTED MY CLOTHES, I'VE HAD TO WEAR A HUGE CLOAK AROUND.
THEY MESSED MY OUTFIT UP SO BADLY, I'LL NEED TO ASK SOMEONE WITH A REALLY HIGH TAILORING SKILL TO FIX IT...
HEH HEH HEH!
UM... RIKA-SAN?

AS A MATTER OF FACT...
...THE GREAT RIKA HAS PROCURED A LEAD THAT YOU MIGHT FIND INTEREST-ING!
OOH! REALLY!?
POKON (BOP)
ポコン
YEOW!
WHAT DO YOU MEAN? EXPLAIN!
HEE-HEE, WELL...
REMEMBER ASHLEY-SAN, FROM SAO?
THE BRILLIANT SEAMSTRESS WHO MAXED OUT THE TAILORING SKILL!?
IS ASHLEY-SAN PLAYING ALO NOW?
YEP, AND I BET YOU CAN ASK HER TO REPAIR YOUR CLOTHES.

ASUNA USED TO CALL ON ASHLEY-SAN DURING THE SAO DAYS ALL THE TIME, AND SO...
I JUST RAN INTO HER AT RANDOM IN ALO. ♪
SHE'S MASTERED THE TAILORING SKILL HERE TOO. WANT ME TO TELL HER ABOUT YOU?
...SHE OFFERED TO SET US UP.
I'VE GOT TO DO REHAB IN THE DOCTOR'S OFFICE, SO GOOD LUCK WITH GYM.
RIKA-SAN, YOU'RE ACTING LIKE YOU DID ALL OF THIS YOURSELF...
...BUT IT SOUNDS TO ME LIKE THIS IS THANKS TO ASUNA-SAN.
JIIII (STARE)
HEY, I CAN TAKE CREDIT FOR WHATEVER MY FRIENDS DO. IT'S WHAT SHARING'S ALL ABOUT!
HEE HEE.
HA HA HA!
ARGH...
IT'S GOOD TO KNOW, THOUGH, RIGHT? WE HAVE TOMORROW OFF.
WANNA INVITE SUGUHA AND GO SEE HER?
YEAH!
WHY DON'T WE MEET UP AT MY HOUSE AND LOG IN?

I'VE ALWAYS WANTED TO HAVE A GIRLS' HANGOUT SO WE CAN LOG IN TOGETHER.
I MEAN, I KNOW IT DOESN'T MAKE A DIFFERENCE WHERE WE LOG IN FROM.

YEAH, THAT SOUNDS FUN.
HOW ABOUT YOU, HIYORI?
I JUST FOUND A GREAT CAKE SHOP, SO I CAN SPLURGE FOR ONE!
YES, I WANT TO SEE KEIKO-SAN'S HOUSE!

WE'LL MEET AT KEIKO'S TOMORROW, THEN!
I'LL INVITE SUGUHA-SAN!
PIPPII (FWEET)
GATHER 'ROUND, GIRLS!

HUH?

SUGUHA-SAN!
YOU'RE KIRITO-SAMA...ER, SAN'S SISTER!?
Y-YEAH, YOU MIGHT SAY THAT.
ZUI (LEAN)
I DIDN'T KNOW WHEN TO BRING IT UP.
GASHI (SNAG)

ZUI (CLEAN)
NEXT TIME WE SHOULD LOG IN AT SUGUHA-SAN'S HOUSE!
H-HUH!?
KYURAN (SPARKLE)
OOOOH, AT SUGUHA'S HOUSE?
THAT SOUNDS LIKE FUN!
AH!
W-WAIT, YOU GUYS! WHAT ARE YOU THINKING!?

WELL, DON'T YOU WANT TO GO SNOOPING AT WHAT'S UNDERNEATH HIS BED...?
OR ELSE-WHERE?
N-NO!

NOPE! NO WAY! ABSOLUTELY NOT!
I MUST PROTECT...
...ONII-CHAN'S SECRETS!
HEE-HEE-HEE...
HA-HA, I'M JUST KIDDING, SUGUHA.
OR HAVE YOU ALREADY SEARCHED DOWN THERE FOR YOURSELF?
NOW THAT I'VE HAD MY FUN AT SUGUHA'S EXPENSE...
...SHALL WE GO IN?
GOOD IDEA.
OF COURSE I HAVEN'T!
KIRITO-SAN...
SUGUHA-CHAN'S SO CUTE.
OH!
I'M SORRY.
I'LL BE A LITTLE BIT LATE. CAN YOU WAIT FOR ME IN THE GAME?
?

I WANT ...
...TO START A BRAND-NEW CHARACTER FROM SCRATCH.
HUH?
WHAT ABOUT KURO?
KURO IS THE PART OF ME THAT SEEKS A "LONELY STRENGTH," THE KIND THAT KIRITO-SAN HAS.
BUT NOW, I'VE LEARNED THAT HIS STRENGTH ISN'T REALLY LIKE THAT.
PLUS I DON'T WANT TO CONFUSE ANYONE WHO ACTUALLY KNOWS HIM, LIKE YOU.

BESIDES, I DECIDED THAT I WANT TO PLAY THE GAME WITH YOU AS MYSELF.
HI-YORI...
WHAT IF YOU DECIDED TO CARRY OVER YOUR SAO CHARACTER DATA?
MY SAO DATA...
IS THAT POSSIBLE?
YES!
THAT'S HOW WE GOT OUR CURRENT CHARACTERS.
REMEMBER WHAT YOU SAID AT SCHOOL? OUR GAME CHARACTERS LOOK JUST LIKE OUR REAL SELVES.
But... I don't, because I never went to SAO...
SHUN (WILT)
YOU'RE JUST FINE THE WAY YOU ARE, AS LEAFA-CHAN!
GAHH!
YOU LOOK SO CUTE WITH THAT BLONDE PONYTAIL AND EVERY-THING!
DO I?

BUT...
...WOULDN'T IT BE NICE TO CARRY OVER YOUR OLD AVATAR AND BRING ALL THE MEMORIES WITH YOU?
OH!
I-I-I'M SORRY!
I FORGOT, YOU LOST YOUR FRIEND...
ばっ
BA (WHOOSH)
NO, IT'S OKAY. THANKS, SUGUHA-SAN.
LOTS OF STUFF HAPPENED, IT'S TRUE...

BUT THERE WERE PLENTY...
...OF MEMORIES I NEVER WANT TO FORGET.

I'VE MADE UP MY MIND.
I THINK I'LL PORT OVER MY SAO SAVE DATA.

WILL YOU WAIT FOR ME IN SWILVANE?
I DECIDED THAT IF I SWITCH OVER, I WANT TO BE A SYLPH.

HIYO-RI...
ALL RIGHT, WE GET IT.

WE'LL
MEET UP IN
SWILVANE.

KURO.
...THANK YOU.

CHIRIN (JINGLE)
Now transferring existing character data to game.
IT'S ALL RIGHT.
IT'S NOT THAT GAME OF DEATH WAITING FOR ME ANY-MORE.
THIS TIME, IT'S A BRIGHT FUTURE WITH SILICA, LIZ, AND LEAFA...

CHIRIN (JINGLE)
チリーン…
IT'S SURE TAKING HIYORI A WHILE...
ARGH, I REALLY AM A MESS...
SO SHE WON'T LOOK LIKE KURO-SAN ANYMORE...
ARE YOU UPSET ABOUT THAT?
Well, it will be weird to interact with the same person in a different character...

...AHA!
POU (GLOW)
HERE SHE COMES.
FUWA (POOF)

パキーン
PAKIN (CRAKK)
HUH?
トッ
TO (TAP)
SILICA, LIZ, LEAFA.
THANKS FOR WAITING.
IF YOU PLEASE...
...THIS AVATAR'S NAME IS "LUX."
A PLEA-SURE TO MEET YOU AGAIN.

?
IS SOME-THING THE MATTER?

Y-YOU TALK DIFFERENT...

HUH?
OH, THAT'S BEEN MY STYLE IN VR, EVEN BEFORE KURO.

Is it... weird?

KUSU (GIGGLE)
HUH? IS IT...REALLY WEIRD!?

UH, SORRY, SORRY.
I WAS WORRIED YOU'D BE COMPLETELY DIFFERENT AFTER CONVERTING...
...BUT YOU'RE JUST AS MUCH KURO-SAN AS YOU EVER WERE. I'M RELIEVED.
OOPS! I MEAN, LUX-SAN!
THANKS, SILICA.
WELL, YOU DEFINITELY THREW ME FOR A LOOP WHEN I MET YOU IN REAL LIFE FOR THE FIRST TIME.
I GUESS YOU'RE THE TYPE WHO TAKES ON A NEW PERSON-ALITY WHEN YOU GET A USERNAME!
HMMM.
DO YOU THINK SO?
PIRA (FLIP)
HYAAAA!

......?
I COULD HAVE SWORN I SAW SOMETHING...
LEAFA!? WH-WHAT WAS THAT FOR!?
WA WA
AH! AWA WA
WA!
BA (SNATCH)
ばっ
Huh? Um...I...
N-NO, IT'S NOT LIKE THAT! I WAS JUST...
SEXUAL HARASSMENT IS BAD, LEAFA.
N-NO, THAT'S NOT WHAT I—!
YEAH, YEAH.
QUIT GOOFING AROUND, OR I'LL LEAVE YOU BEHIND.

TO (HOP)
トッ
AH! HANG ON.
C'MON...
YOU DON'T UNDER-STAND!
LET'S GO FLY TO SEE ASHLEY-SAN!

To be continued in the next volume!

BY THE WAY, LUX-SAN...
...WHY DID YOU HOLD THE SWORDS BACKWARD FROM THE WAY KIRITO-SAN DID WHEN YOU WERE PLAYING AS KURO-SAN?
AFTERWORD MANGA
"SILICA'S QUESTION"
BY: NEKO NEKOBYOU

HUH?
BACK-WARD?

YES.

kirito
kuro
HE CARRIED THE WHITE BLADE IN HIS LEFT HAND AND THE BLACK ONE IN HIS RIGHT.
I NOTICED YOU DID IT THE OTHER WAY AROUND, LIKE A MIRROR IMAGE.
I WAS WONDERING IF THERE WAS SOME KIND OF MEANING BEHIND THAT.

FURU (TREMBLE)
FURU
Ah! Sorry!
ACK!
If you'd rather not say...

I HAD IT...
...BACK-WARD?

SHE'S A DITZ!!!
HYAAAA! BUT I CHECKED IN THE MIRROR AND EVERY-THING...!!!
THAT'S WHY!!

YAJI

REKI KAWAHARA-SENSEI
(THANKS FOR USING THE ANGEL'S WHISPER RING IDEA IN YOUR PINA EDITION DOUJINSHI! I'LL TREASURE IT FOREVER!)

ABEC-SENSEI

KAZUMI MIKI-SAMA

TOMOYUKI TSUCHIYA-SAMA

EVERYONE WHO READ THIS BOOK!

IT'S OUR TURN NOW!

MoRE
DEBAN
APPEARANCES

SWORD ART ONLINE: GIRLS' OPS 1

ORIG

Translation: Stephen Paul
Lettering: Brndn Blakeslee & Lys Blakeslee

This book is a work of fiction. Names, characters, places, and incidents are the product of the author's imagination or are used fictitiously. Any resemblance to actual events, locales, or persons, living or dead, is coincidental.

Edited by ASCII MEDIA WORKS
First published in Japan in 2014 by KADOKAWA CORPORATION, Tokyo.
English translation rights arranged with KADOKAWA CORPORATION, Tokyo, through Tuttle-Mori Agency, Inc., Tokyo.

Yen Press
Hachette Book Group
1290 Avenue of the Americas
New York, NY 10104

www.HachetteBookGroup.com
www.YenPress.com

Yen Press is an imprint of Hachette Book Group, Inc. The Yen Press name and logo are trademarks of Hachette Book Group, Inc.

The publisher is not responsible for websites (or their content) that are not owned by the publisher.

First Yen Press Edition: May 2015

ISBN: 978-0-316-34205-6

10 9 8 7 6 5 4 3 2 1

BVG

Printed in the United States of America